The Penny Farthing STORIES

BRIAN J. H. SLACK

AuthorHouse™ UK Ltd.
1663 Liberty Drive
Bloomington, IN 47403 USA
www.authorhouse.co.uk
Phone: 0800.197.4150

Published by AuthorHouse 04/25/2014

ISBN: 978-1-4918-9767-6 (sc)
ISBN: 978-1-4918-9768-3 (e)

authorHOUSE®

The
Come-uppance

Almost a Novel

You don't have to be that handsome
To be a lady's man.
You can do without the tall, dark bit
And striving for a tan.

Mister Hippo Potts, the bon viveur
Of independent means,
Had no difficulty whatsoever,
Surprising though it seems.
At first glance, you'd think him fat;
On that, you would be wrong.
'Twas muscle, no flab at all,
Short, stout, and very strong.
True, he had a massive head
With tiny, piercing eyes.
An enormous mouth, convenient
For telling whopping lies.
All those who knew about him
Heard that he was rich.
Ah! And what a difference that would make
To any scheming bitch.
Dapper in a well-cut suit,
A jaunty bowler hat,
A gold watch chain, and walking cane;
Haute couture with spats.
When all dolled up resplendent,
He'd sally forth up west.

3

Of all the evening's pleasures,
He liked the theatre best.
Loved it! Would go twice a week;
The stage was life itself.
Often he would take a box
And fill it with himself.
Oh! The music, lights, and glamour;
The line of chorus girls;
The dancing and the show of legs;
The frivolity and twirls.
He swore it blew his cobwebs off,
Put twinkles in his eye,
A certain cure when peckers drooped;
And one can quite see why.
A final swishing of the curtain,
The dying of applause;
The jostling backstage Johnnies
Blocking up the doors.
But Hippo Potts just
sauntered through.
He never had to ask,
For everyone excused him,
Stood aside and let him pass.

His appearance in the dressing rooms
Caused bustling of delight,
For he always chose six pretty ones
To take out for the night.
"Oh! What larks! Our
luck has changed!
"No fear of nuffin shady,
"'Cos only them what's proper toffs
"Knows 'ow to treat a liedy!"
Hair and attire quickly fixed,
Their face's paint repaired,
And snatching up handbags and hats
Skipped blithely down the stairs.
They clambered into hackney cabs,
Excited by the treat,
The clattering horse's lively pace.
"Gee up! Tonight we eat!"

At Calorelli's Supper Rooms,
The smartest place in town,
A good blow-out of haute cuisine
And champs to wash it down.

Then liqueurs with slaps and giggles,
A tippling of gin;
They were ever so appreciative
And nearly smothered him.
His large, full-blooded, sensual lips
Wrapped halfway round his head;
Where others kiss just one at once,
He managed six instead.
The most tactful of arrangements,
As no one felt denied;
Whilst kissing two in front of him,
Kissed two on either side.
The coquettish battle then commenced,
Feline-like and grim,
It brought out all the worst in them
And all their best for him.

One Tilly Poodle stole the march;
Her stage name was Valetta.
With chosen, prepared fine cigar,
Resolved he'd know her better.
Alighting gently on his knee,
Her head upon his chest,
Tickling his fancy and his ear,
Disinheriting the rest.
With titillating bills and coos,
She assessed her treasure.

Oh her, "Uncle-wuncle sugar ducks!"
His face reddened with pleasure.
Keenly collaring his patronage.
By using woman's wiles,
Left the others masquerading,
Disguising spite with smiles.
Her coup d'état: accomplished.
The perks to be supplied,
But Tilly was a shameless slut:
— A lover on the side!

7

Perhaps 'lover' was too strong a word
For one so short of puff.
A few days labouring down the docks
Proved far more than enough.
So sensitively dedicated
To all the pains he had;
Just to mention that word 'work'
Would bring his back on, bad.
In all truth, it must be said,
His front wasn't any fitter,
For he'd grown a brewer's belly
By downing pints of bitter.
Expensive gifts were promptly pawned.
Flushed with the money sent,
They both lived very comfortably,
No worries about rent.
They together made a right good pair.
If lamp of truth were lit,
He'd prove nothing but a hippo
And she a hippocrite.
Being one of this world's takers
And his trust usurped,
While milking him for all she's worth,
Said, "Pottsie is a twerp!"
She played him false, the hussy.
— He found out! — She had her chips.
He crunched her up in his big mouth
And spat her out in bits.

'Twas something she would not forget.
Pity about the pain,
But it taught her a sharp lesson,
And she'd not do that again.
One can sympathize with him, of course,
For feeling narked inside.
All that attention, and now this?
It hurts a fellow's pride.
He knew he should not dwell on it
And deprive himself of bliss,
For by way of consolation,
He still had five to kiss.

The Hon. R. M. Da Higham

Rudolphus Mark Da Higham:
A giraffe of noble lineage
Whose ancestors did not resort
To murder, burn, or pillage.
His father was none other than
The Earl of Tallington.
The family seat was Upney Park,
But more of that anon.
As third in line had little chance
Of title or estate
With elder brother's families,
However long he'd wait.
This left him with no option
But to make his way in life,
Succeeding – or failing, find
An heiress for a wife.
He was completely at a loss
What his career should be;
Of necessity, commensurate
With his august family.
First choice was the regiment but
Not granted a commission.
Being too tall for the trenches
Would pinpoint their position.

A frightful pity, don't you know?

Should he perhaps pick up the pen?
A man of letters be:
A poet, an author – some epic work,
A family history?
A desperate search for inspiration,
He furiously scratched and scribbled
Till finally his muse came down to
Box his ears for writing drivel.

Oh dear, not his vocation, obviously!

This only seemed to leave the church;
Perhaps this was to be his calling?
But Uncle Theodore pointed out,
Despite the years of training,
It would ruin the whole effect
Of being piously aloof
If he climbed into a pulpit and
Banged his head against the roof.

Ah well, that's that then!

'Twas not for want of trying,
But despair was pressing hard.
For relief, he'd try as exercise
A solemn promenade.

One day, whilst thus meandering,
He was startled by a clatter,
Whereupon he turned round sharp
To see what was the matter.
And there burst forth upon him
Awe and wonder at the sight
Of gorillas going great guns
On their penny-farthing bikes.

He leapt aside as they flashed past,
Each formidably robust,
Vanishing as quickly as they came,
Leaving swirling clouds of dust.
Winded, stunned, and excited by
That amazing turn of speed
Produced a sudden revelation
And the planting of a seed.
"Good gracious me, how wonderful!
Could I, should I? But no.
But then again, why ever not?
By Jove, I'll have a go!"
Life's prospects opened up for him;
That damned career could wait.
He'd have that bike whatever
And put it on the slate.

To Messrs Wobbleton and Judder's
Bicycling establishment
Noted for their bespoke wheels
And knocking out of dents.
Of all their new boneshakers,
It came as a surprise:
There was not even one in stock
To accommodate his size.
They could take specific orders
For whatever he required,
A customized special to
Be very much admired.
As token of esteem agree
To brake, a lamp and bell.
The formalities completed,
A sherry sealed the deal.

So, that was that – the die was cast.
Now he just had to wait
In agonized anticipation
For that delivery date
.

Rudolphus and the servants rushed
Out as the cart arrived
To welcome its precious load
And meet it on the drive.
Off came the crate with willing hands,
The unpackers very keen
To see in revealed magnificence
The glistening machine.
It was enormous when stood up,
With retainers either side
To hold it steady as he climbed
To start his maiden ride.
It was horribly unstable with
His weight so high above.
With his feet upon the pedals,
Others rushed to give a shove.
A start of frightful wobbles,
Hectic careening – fear!
It was hairy stuff to watch as
He struggled hard to steer.
A case of "Ride 'em cowboy!"
Headlong towards the wall.
A near miss with the balustrade,
But still he did not fall.

Disappeared behind the west wing,
—A long and pregnant pause
Till wobbled round the east wing
To a burst of loud applause.
The Earl sat contemplating
With a whisky near at hand.
What passed the first-floor window?
He could not understand.
He fancied he had seen his son,
Though how could not explain,
When a few moments later,
"Ahrra! There he goes again!"
He looked hard at the decanter
As causing his dismay.
"I think that I might just partooked
A nip too much today!"
Around and around the stately pile,
He mastered the bike with glee.
His steed stowed in the stable, then
In Triumph home for tea.

Next morn: breakfast early,
Asked to leave the table,
Eager to be up and out, rushed
Over to the stable.
And there it was. Ah, what a joy!
"It's still there and ready.
"Quick, call the grooms to roll it out,
"Assist, and hold it steady."
Propped up by stable staff,
Precarious on his perch,
Then off with a cheer and on his way,
Surviving that first lurch.

The thrill of riding also had
An unexpected treat:
Things looked freshly different from
His mobile vantage seat.
Over the hedge, he was now aware
Of the trimmed parterre's design.
The blooms atop the pergola
Looked particularly fine.
Past the dolphin fountain, though,
Too early to be playing,
A glimpse of rich herbaceous-ness
As his speed was gaining.
The landscape then expanding,
With just a fleeting sight
Of the cascade and the grotto
Way over to the right.
Over the bridge across the lake,
Whizzing rather fast,
Swinging out around the main gates,
"Ah! The open road at last!"
Three miles and a half to Tallington,
Oh, happy harmony!
Gliding though the rolling country
In joyous symphony,
The steady rhythm of the pedals,
Gentle singing of the wheels.
It seemed he was flying by
Hedges, trees, and fields,
With the bright and skittish clouds
Amid the boisterous blow:
The most glorious of bestest days!
Now only one to go.

Both he and we must pause to tell
Of what the world would see
That beggars all description by
Lesser men than me:
Silk-lapelled inserts on his coat,
Kid gloves, a neat cravat,
A white carnation freshly picked,
A tall black silk top hat,
Recalling Salisbury's wondrous spire.
All of five "wows!" high
As the grand English perpendicular
Serenely passed them by.

Astonished townsfolk gasped in awe;
Some bobbed or doffed instead.
In deference to effulgence,
A vicar bared his head.
Courteously considerate, he
Glided through the town
Wealth's responsibilities kept
The revolutions down.

He proved a natural rider,
Did things others learn;
He used his tail instinctively
To indicate a turn.
In meritorious restraint till
He reached the boundary stone,
With all the local traffic gone,
The road was now his own.
Now, the chance and powerful urge
Itching to be trying

To see what he and bike could do to
Set his coat-tails flying.
Thrilled, excited beyond words – such
Adventurous progression,
An athletic experience which
Grew to an obsession.
Now rarely seen at home,
His absence caused concern.
Her Ladyship called the butler,
His whereabouts to learn.
She oft inquired in languorous tones,
"Have you seen my darling?"
"He's been and gone again, milady,
On his penny-farthing."
What paradox, the painful pleasure:
Straining, short of breath,
Enjoying pedalling for dear life
Whilst shaken half to death.
The wildest claims abounded by
Those who loved to spin it,
Emphatic they'd seen him shift at
Thirty strewths a minute.
The young thought he was wonderful.
The old, stark raving mad.
The middle-aged, a bit of both,
His example poor to bad.
If this was all he ever did,
'Twas waste of public school.
But what *profanum vulgus* thought
Concerned him not at all.

Then one day – one dreadful day,
He thought he would explore
And take a different route to ride
That he'd not tried before.
At first, all things went splendidly,
Till he came up to a ramp.
And from a bar athwart the road,
There swung a red-eyed lamp.
Some declared this was an omen,
Made portentualistic claims;
In actual fact, the reason was they
Were digging up the drains.
The obstruction caused Rudolphus to
Proceed by turning right.
He soon picked up lost speed again
And came upon the sight
Of a glorious sweep of country in
The valley there below.
From a hill crest he descended,
It alluring him to go
Faster at no effort with his
Feet clear for freewheeling,
Sailing though the gentle curves,
Feeling just like singing.
Whizzing, flying down the hill
And flashing round a bend,
Travelling in the grandest style
To his untimely end.
A railway bridge stood in his path,
Too low to let him through.
Far too fast! He closed his eyes;
There was nowt else he could do.

He struck the arch a fearful thwack.
Instant was his ending;
Grasping crossbar to the last,
With the wheels still spinning.

Such shock and consternation,
A state of disbelief
Were responses to the news
Of unplacated grief.
So much clearing up to do
Of this most ghastly mess –
Arrangements in profusion
Before he's laid to rest.
Those with prophetic powers
Cried, "There, I told you so!"
That they could see it coming made
Sure everyone would know.
Full coverage of the tragedy
Appearing in the press.
Descriptions and announcements
Helped keep one abreast
With pages on the funeral,
Its pomp and eulogies.

The massive crowds attended
The service and high teas;
Later, a quiet interment in the
Family mausoleum
To join his noble forebears
Reverentially beside them.
Of course they held an inquest
To rightly ascertain
The precise cause of death
And to whom apportion blame,
Detailed medical evidence
Was given by a prof:
"The rest of him is of no use if
The top bit's got knocked off."
Death by misdirection was
The verdict of the court.
"A vital recommendation,"
Concluded the report.
The facts of this disastrous
Incident require
Government to order railway
Bridges to be higher.

In the verdant vistas of
The Upney Park estate,
A hillock with a screen of trees
That sweeps down to the lake:
The site chosen to erect a
Temple to Joyous Speed.
Its design incorporated
Parts of his much-loved steed.
The rim of the large penny wheel
Was laid upon six columns.
The farthing wheel placed above
On curved wrought-iron arms.
Topped by a gilded Hermes
That glistens in the sun,
Sacred to the memory of
Their late, lamented son.

When the moon's in its first quarter,
Saturn in Orion's belt,
And those things that are
unknowable
But are most keenly felt;
When the wind is sou'-sou'-east
No sorry! nor'-nor'-west –
Not that it really matters much;
Whichever blows the best?
For screaming through the tortured
trees –
Wild clouds upon the march,
A timely flash of lightning
Illumes a railway arch.

A swirling, swerving, whirling,
A faint tinkling of a bell,
And he's rising high above you,
Having pedalled up from hell.
One acknowledges the standard size
Of ghosts and of ghouls,
But this monstrous apparition
Is most horror-ibly tall.
Those unfortunate to see it are
Left mentally deranged,
Brings on convulsive shaking
When handling small change.

Oh, please don't look so frightened!
Rest assured and realise,
A legend is another word
For just a pack of lies.

IMPEDED

A Mere Farthing's worth

Pity the poor centipede;
To call him dim is cruel.
It's finding fifty pairs of shoes
That makes him late for school.
It's all right for us with two feet;
We can afford to laugh.
But agony with a hundred
Getting into a hot bath.
It's ten times worse for millipedes –
Far worse in every way.
One wonders why they don't give up
And stay in bed all day.
I would not want to run the risk
Of spoiling every treat,
Sploshing though a muddy puddle –
Takes hours to wipe your feet.
Just trying on new trousers
Requires teeth-grinding grit:
Struggling into all those legs
To find they do not fit!
He has unexpected talents
That one would not suppose;
It's very clever he can use
His toes to blow his nose.
How boring, being so profound
With all those feet upon the ground.

The Ballad of Hamish MacHoots

Wee Hamish MacHoots was a Scottish hedgehog
Employed by the Laird of Lockey
To play bagpipes and marbles to entertain guests
Whom the Laird had invited to tea.
But he'd only dare play the saddest laments,
For when he played wild, highland reels
He'd get over excited, pump far too hard,
And puncture his bag with his quills.
His long, dreary dirges invariably drew
Disobedient tears from the guests.
Drops trickled on the fronts of their shirts
And soaked through to their vests.
They cried on the cream cakes; they soggied the scones;
They wailed, and they wetted the fudge.
The trifles were ruined, and so were the tarts;
The shortbreads dissolved into sludge.
In vain did wet handkerchiefs try to dry eyes.
Blown noses were glowing, red raw,
Till exhausted and panting, fell back in their chairs.
They just could not take anymore!

The Laird was distracted, aggrieved, and dismayed,
His puffed eyes as red as a cherry.
He just did not know what to say to his guests
Tried so awfully hard to be merry.
The food was so scrumptious, so sticky, and so rich,
And the Laird so genteel and well bread,
But emotionally drained, they vowed, "Never again!"
And made their excuses and fled.
Oh dear!

Then one day, from the south, came a mouse with a mouth
That could murder a nice cup of tea.
He preferred a dry shirt and was very alert –
And had wits as quick as a flea.

He spotted the reason why Hamish played slow,
The pumping confined to low gears.
It seemed such a shame: only hungry ones came,
With cotton wool stuffed in their ears.
For a solution, he sought for a thought
To speed up the huffing and puffing.
As he pondered some more while pacing the floor,
He'd a brainwave whilst scoffing at a muffin.
"By thunder, I've got it!" in triumph he cried.
For he certainly knew he was right
Then bellowed his devious plan in each ear;
Their eyes lit up bright in delight!
They leapt up from table, a scattering chairs
As they made for the door with a roar.
So great was the rush, some were caught in the crush
And picked themselves up from the floor.
Like thunder, they tore along long corridors.
The rumpus caused footmen to panic;
One gave in his notice right there and then
And returned to his mother in Alnwick.
Like stampeding bison, they stormed down the stairs;
Cook locked herself in, fearfully flurried.
Swerving round banisters, sliding down rails,
With wild, helter-skelter, they hurried
To the grim suit of armour that gloweringly scowled
'Cause his job was so boring to do.

He'd been on guard duty for six hundred years
Protecting those using the loo.
With feverish frenzy, hands took him apart;
It was all such splendiferous fun!
They all grabbed a piece with great yelps of delight
And reran the race they had run.
Oh . . . dear!
Oh dear, oh dear!

Poor Hamish, meantime, gawped and agogged.
His bagpipes hung slumped at his side.
Fixed rigid in terror at what they might do,
Too afraid to think quickly to hide.
He'd heard all the uproar go fading away
To the distant parts of the hall –
In horror, heard them coming back like a train,
Screaming like banshees an' all.
Louder and nearer, rampaging, they came.
The ominous coming of doom,
Wee Hamish just shivered and quavered and quivered,
Overwhelmed as they burst in the room.
The mob, now determined to fix him for good,
Ignoring his piteous pleas.
To put paid to his wail, they encased him in mail
With a shirt that reached down to his knees.
They clamped on the breastplate and piece for his back.
That produced a slight squeal of alarm,
So they wedged on the helmet right over his head
And clipped on the bits for his arms.

Though dusty and rusty, it sort of did fit;
At least they would see if it worked.
And shoving the bagpipes up under his arm,
They bonked his hard hat if he shirked.
He found he could pump just as hard as liked
And whip up a fair head of steam.
The armour did rattle a clamorous clank,
Which everyone thought was a scream.
He was happy to please with this devilish wheeze,
With music both lively and glad.
They demanded some more by shouting, "Encore!"
And thumping the table like mad.
They rushed to make sets for the dance of a jig
That he played at a deuce of a lick.
They leapt and they swung and laughed and they sang
While the Laird beat the time with his stick.
The fleet-footed capered, and the scissor-legged leaped
Over crossed swords, wee drams, and a haggis.
They yelled their dismay at the flashy display
Of the real clever stuff of the braggist.

Some danced with a hand on the side of their waist
To swankily show they were able,
Refuting suggestions they'd caught indigestion
From rising too quickly from table.
They danced and they frolicked; they pranced and they rollicked
Till the wee beastie hours of the night.
When they'd had quite enough, they just shut off his puff
By slamming his visor down tight.
But oh, what a *ceilidh* and rare time they had.
Ough! What whoopsily dizzily heads!
All knackeredly tired but happy as Larry
As each tottered home to their beds.

But early next morning, they're up with the lark
And grabbing whoever they met
To tell them the tale of the glorious time,
Of the night they would never forget.
The news raced apace like a forest on fire.
High society, cunning as ever,
Started once more to attend on the Laird
No matter whatever the weather.

With every good reason, the height of the season's
Most fashionable thing was the dance;
If you wished to be seen sipping tea at Lockey,
You had to book months in advance.
They sent begging letters, or plead at the gates
Trying hard to procure invitations.
There were crowds for them now because they were free.
Then they sold them to friends and relations.
The kindly old Laird did his best for his friends,
But the withdrawing room proved too small.
He laid out more plates; put more tea in the pot,
And repaired to the banqueting hall.
The high tea and high jinks are held once a week
With highland jigs, flings things and reels
Attracting fine carriages, bulging with fans for
This hell of a fella in steel.
For wonderful Hamish is famous at last:
A legend! An idol! A star!
His armour's been buffed up and fits like a glove,
And everyone knows he'll go far.

He's now highly polished, this bright but small knight
At the start of a brilliant career.
And swaggers about with a dignified pride,
Looking really mag fab in his gear,
With sashes of tartan and buckles and belt
And a colourful plume that is fit for
A noble, high-spirited Liberty horse,
That's stuck right on top of his titfer.
What a dashing, romantic, fine figure he makes.
The ladies just swoon at his entry.
His gauntleted fingers inspire o'er the pipes
That's the envy of all of the gentry.
But it's not widely known that his image is helped
By the fact they've enclosed every prickle;
He now always plays with a smile on his face —
Each movement he makes don't half tickle!

THE CAMPAIGNS OF GENERALISSIMO CROCODELLO IN LOVE AND WAR

In the mighty delta of the Youkertager River,
In the rushes by the bandstand in the park,
Lived a baby crocodile who had such a lovely smile
And liked to go a-hunting in the dark.
He learnt to be quiet as he lay down in the mud
And waited till his dinner paddled by.
He'd suddenly go, "Boo!" which is very rude – it's true.
Then he'd gobble them before they'd time to cry.
His name was Vassellaygo el Certoweser Sagermourai
Del Frandangous Santa Anna de har Med
Don Quiehentey Crocodello, with the accent on the *e*
And that's why everybody called him Fred.
His father was ambitious for the honour of his house,
Driven by heroic visions of the troops
That his son would lead to glory made the old crock very happy
Couldn't stand your namby-pambey nincompoops.

The baby in due season grew up big to be a boy,
He thought a rough and tumbles such a wheeze.
He learnt useful battle tactics having skirmishes with sharks.
He'd punch them on the nose and make them sneeze.
Father sent him off to college for expertise and knowledge
To lean the arts and subtleties of war.
He stayed there for six years, though his mother was in tears,
And he came home even tougher than before.
In due course, with his commission, he was sent out on a mission
By his nation to a station in the east.
There was trouble in Kertarger in the town of Whatapong:
The Kertargies weren't invited to a feast
That the maharajah gave for the marriage of a slave
Whom he really did not have the right to keep.
He'd procured her from a man who'd acquired her in Japan –
He had pinched her while her master was asleep.
I need not, of course, remind you of the trouble that it caused.
It made headlines in all the papers,
A devilish to do indeed if all's to be believed
Of the fascinating details of his capers.
Suffice it here to say, that young Crocky won the day;
To-day you know it's tactics that's the thing
Showed them how to bang a gun, got the rebels on the run,
And got a medal for his trouble, from the King.
He was proclaimed a hero, and quite right, for he'd shown guts.
He was hopelessly outnumbered from the start,
But he used a brilliant ruse and slipped tin tacks in their shoes.
And their battle lines just simply fell apart.

There were those who proposed statues and passed around
The bowler hat, every penny to perpetuate his fame.
In unprecedented latitude, the government in gratitude
Bestowed the highest rank; and now his name
Is Generalissimo Vassellaygo el Certoweser Sagermourai
Del Frandangous Santa Anna de har Med
Don Quiehentey Crocodello, with the accent on the *e*
And no one ever dares to call him Fred,
Oh! No indeed.

As he crossed the sands of Egypt at the head of all his men,
Which, as you know, is phewie hot and very sunny,
He met a gorgeous camel and promptly fell in love;
Which his army thought was very, very funny.
It was difficult to tell her, the short-legged little fella
Found it hard to reach up high enough to kiss,
Till one day she sat and posed with her yashmak on her nose.
It was not an opportunity to miss.
As she gently lowered her neck, he gave her a little peck.
He had the bliss of it, not once but twice.
Remember, if you scoff: he could have bit it off.
So, really, he was being very nice.
As they quietly puffed their hashish, it surprised him when she spoke
Spanish
That she'd picked up on a trip to Santiago.
Her name was Semolina; she could dance the tapioca
And learnt the macaroni flute in Costa Sago.

She was very, very pretty. Although he wasn't, he was witty;
Mumbled lovey-dovey doings in her ear;
Never felt like this before – couldn't bother with the war.
Could all this mean the end of his career?
His heart was all a-flutter, melted like a knob of butter
That made a greasy mess of all his schemes.
Should he issue a decree? Send his soldiers home for tea?
But he didn't 'cause he was lost in all his dreams.
He crocol ogle eyed her and canoodled there beside her
And referred to all the stars in his advances.
He plied her with the pride of pickings of his plundered loot,
He certainly was not taking any chances.
With diamond rings and necklaces and other costly jewels,
That he put into a casket with a key.
He tied on a charming note, for with a quill he wrote:
"With ever loving thoughts, to you, from me."
The poor maid was overcome by the way he shook his bum
And flicked out all the creases from his tail.
He said he grieved to leave her but must go on his campaigning.
At this, she let out such a tragic wail.

He pretended to be sad but inside was very glad,
For he knew that he had got her at his feet,
Quiet certain she would yearn for the day of his return.
The conquest of his love was now complete.
So putting on his hat, he thought, "That's quite enough of that!
"There's a battle to be won against the Kaiser."
Then he bade her good day and marched off on his way.
Though how, or where, or why, we're none the wiser.
He did not, of course, forget her but in fact proposed by letter
Written amidst cannon's thunderous roars.
So dramatically emphatic, Semolina was ecstatic.
Wrote him, "Yes!" And thus began her wifely chores
As Mrs Vassellaygo el Certoweser Sagermourai
Del Frandangous Santa Anna de har Med
Don Quiehentey Crocodello, with the accent on the *e*.
There is very little more now to be said.
They settled down in Nice by invitation of the mayor,
Who bowed very low to both and called him sir.
They live in a splendid mansion built across a stream:
That is wet enough for him and high for her.

At half past ten each morning on the dot till five past twelve,
He parades his army up and down the square,
It causes such a havoc as it holds up all the traffic,
He just couldn't give a toss and doesn't care.
Little kiddies peep and giggle between their parents' legs
As they meet with friends and stay to have long talks,
He's got a funny wiggle that starts somewhere in the middle,
And he tends to run a little when he walks.
So there you are, my lovelies, my story has been told.
By this time, you should really know his name.
But in case you have not got it, I will give you one more chance
To get it right, so here we go again.
It's Generalissimo Vassellaygo el Certoweser Sagermourai
Del Frandangous Santa Anna de her Med
Don Quiehentey Crocodello, with the accent on the –
Ho, I've had enough of this – I'm off to bed!

Gold Snow and the High Trestle

Striking gold in Konnit Mountain caused more trouble than you'd think,
For there's nothing like the yellow stuff for whipping up a stink.
The merest sniff or whisper sparks enough to detonate
A blast of man's worst passions in his fight to change his fate.
Those with steady jobs and families would throw down their tools
And rushed headlong aside of felons, vagrants, and fools,
All scrambling in highest hopes but very little else,
Banking on Dame Fortune in their ruthless dash for wealth.

It sparkled in stupendous grandeur of a country that belonged
Out in the lonely wilds at the back edge of beyond.
Amid forests of sweet-smelling pines, high hills, and rocky ranges,
A trapper gathering skins and pelts, who'd been up there for ages,
A one-eyed bear, a grizzly, an old timer past his prime.
Still not one to mess with – you'd be dead before your time.
As for his name, that no one knew, if even one he had.
Elks would holler, "Old Big Grizz," then wisely run like mad.
As a hermit hunter, he'd lived completely on his own.
For two years, the vast wilderness had been his only home.
Whilst hunting in a mountain pass he spotted, just by chance,
Yellow sparkles in a stream that caused Big Grizz to dance.
Most excitedly, he raked about. Were more grains in the ground?
‑—‑—‑—‑—‑—‑—‑—‑—‑—"YIPPEE!"
His mind: ablaze with what to do with the gold he'd found.
Scrouting amongst the banks and boulders – peering, poking, pulling:
Just as well no one could see or know what he was doing.

He'd caught the fever big time, the malaria of lust.
Another stone was overturned, and waters rinsed the dust
And there revealed the peeping tip of a gleaming nugget.
He prised it from its bed in joy and hid it in his pocket!

The timing worked out very well, with the weather due to change.
If he appeared in town with pelts, no one would think it strange.
He resolved to close his camp and bundled up his skins,
Which he hung from either side and dangled to his shins.
Packed provisions and his gun were slung across his back.
Followed the stream through rocky woods for three weeks on the trek.

It led him to the Itchyswitch, a river vigorously flowing.
Needing rafts for shooting rapids and five days of hard going,
The river carried and swirled him into Grunter's Creek,
Where he broke his journey to rest his poor old feet.

As the furthest point upstream that was reached by a sternwheeler,
All to do was step aboard and take passage on the steamer
For the four days' drop downriver to the port of San Drego.
Two years past, San Drego was very much a no go.

Amazed was he when he stepped ashore to find so much bustle.
Lots of buildings springing up, awful noise and hustle.
First, the fur trading office to settle his account.
Made a good deal for the quality, condition, and amount
Of pelts he had gathered up in the wild country.
Now, dollar flushed, he needed to be unusually canny.
Outside, the docks were busy with enlargements to the quay,
Unloading of materials that had been brought by sea.
The construction of a railroad that had been talked up for years
Comes as something of a shock when it finally appears.
The San Drego and Wickyappelis line had now hit the town,
Its building had caused things to go up whilst others to came down.

Its railhead, a single track, was laid aside the quay
Then down the middle of Main Street, out to infinity.
From a corner, Big Grizz stopped, startled, to just stare.
Wow! A sizzling loco, belching smoke, standing in the square:
A monstrous fangled thing on wheels, oddly, softly snarling.
He was sure that it was fierce and unpredictably alarming.
Much went on around it, some attending it like bees.
He kept quite clear of the nasty thing to see to his own needs:
Off to the Old Spittoon Saloon, where he'd usually stayed.
'Twas now the Iron Horse Hotel and touting for new trade.
He stepped inside, the place transformed in a sassy style,
Tarted up the joint with paint that reeked of linseed oil.
Mirrors backed a new, long bar with bottles on the shelves.
Gone were the days when one just flicked a coin and helped your selves.
They'd tacked on an extension, set up a roulette wheel.
Where once you had played poker, you now just sat and had a meal.
Plush red curtains, potted palms, and two flashy chandeliers –
Overwhelmed, the swanky changes reduced him near to tears.

What really killed the old days off was a notice on the door,
"No Drunken Brawling Is Allowed nor Spitting on the Floor."
The place was filled up with a gibbon sitting down to plonk
A tinkly, jinkly type of tune upon a honky-tonk.
No way was he used to this; fragile nerves needed a drink.
Big Grizz ordered a beer and chaser, slumped in a chair to think.

A waiter brought his poison. "Please, may I pay for that?
"I can tell, sir, you're a trapper by your Davy Crockett hat."
Grizz turned and saw a lion standing there,
Who raised his hat congenially whilst pulling up a chair.
An impressive presence to be sure, a head blessed with strong features:
A determined mass of wiry hair and glorious side whiskers.
This was Growlerzoon van Roarden, the one who led the team,
Causing all the tumult, and was known as Old Van Steam.

Now the chief engineer of the Drego and Wicky line.
He was courteously affable and invited Grizz to dine.
He expressed his admiration for the trappers' life and knowledge
Of their particular area and ability to forage.
He talked to them, as he needed and valued their advice.
They found it useful to oblige him with such details – for a price.
To join Wickyappelis with the sea had always been its strength,
Whereas the problem of the line had always been its length.
As things now stood, the only way to go was round the mountains,
A loop of four hundred miles and trouble for the trains.
Passing through the native reservation of the Pekocheeks
Guaranteed ambush attacks, running gunfights, and near squeaks.
There was great need to find a route through the high hills;
The success of finding a western pass so far had been nil.
Did he perhaps know of somewhere they could try?
Big Grizz slowly nodded — and gleamed with his one eye.
Highly excited, instantly Van Roarden grabbed his paw,
Pulled him from the table, and rushed him to the door.
Out in the bustling melee of barrels, bales, and flagons,
Nipping between criss-crossing carts and heavy lumbering wagons.
Alongside a railroad carriage, they went to the end, and then
Both climbed the steps to board Van Roarden's mobile den.
An office with a bedroom – most commodious once inside –
And a potbellied stove doing its job marked the great divide.

Scruffling through his papers, piled higgledy on his desk,
He found the map, laid it flat, folded arms upon his chest.
Big Grizz bent over and peered hard; that one eye worked for two.
Then at last, he made a mark, moved it, and followed through.

"Are you sure – really sure? Has it any name whatsoever?"
"Yep! It's called Runny Nose Pass. It'll fit you fine, despite some rotten weather!
"I'd been exploring, setting traps up there on my own
"For all of five months last year and left me handkerchief at home"
Confirming many details, amid intense and long discussion
Of the pass's possibilities for the line's construction.
Agreeing that Big Grizz should give his services and skills,
Employed by the railroad as their man up in the hills,
Making preliminary arrangements for surveying the terrain.
Then Big Grizz asked, "How do you go about registering a claim?"
Van Roarden gasped in horror – for a moment he just froze,
Groaned, and in hushed tones exclaimed, "Not gold in Runny Nose?"

Grizz said, "No, not in the pass."

"That's enough! Do not say more!

"I must not know," regaining the composure he'd displayed before.

Explaining that of all the things he dreaded most to hear,

Are, "There's gold in them there hills!" to a line's chief engineer.

He implored Grizz not to register, or at least not yet.

"Keep it a guarded secret; otherwise, you can bet

"If labouring gangs get wind of it, you may be certain that

"With company picks and shovels, they'd be off like scalded cats.

"As sure as hell not one of them could be induced to stay.

"All work stops – abandoned, not just a delay.

"A disaster! Bruised shareholders refuse to reinvest.

"It could take years to resume the push towards the west.

"Having made such a find, asking so much is tough,

"But what's at stake is make or break. I cannot beg enough!"

Big Grizz had his own problems, handed out by fate.

The finding of the golden hoard came ten years too late.

The prospects of prospecting are quite daunting when you're old.

It's rough enough when you're tough to cope with wet and cold.

He was not sure if his back was up to digging or the fights

That he knew would be inevitable to maintain his rights.

They both recognized the importance of one thing at a time;

Nothing must interfere with the building of the line.

Until then, Grizz agreed to hold fire on his claim

But strike one like greased lightning should some other do the same.

Van Roarden said, "Meanwhile, keep it all hush-hush.

"Then we'll establish Grizzville and make ready for the rush.

"You can't stop the lemmings, though we should help them try.
"I see it as a kindness – nay, our duty – to supply
"Vital vittles, drinks, baccy, jackets, shirts and trousers,
"Tents, shovels, pans, stores, a saloon, and even banking houses,
"Where they can either have gold weighed and sell to us the dust
"Or bring nuggets to deposit in a safe that they can trust.
"Let the rabble dig, swill, and squabble 'mongst themselves
"Whilst we stand aside reliably, keeping well-stocked shelves.

"Inevitably, some will fail – their despair is such a pity –
"While those that pay, we can convey to high-jinks in the city.
"This monopoly should prove a successful undertaking.
"Theirs the scratching for the gold – ours the profit for the raking."
A day in modern business! Who would have ever thought?
At nine, Big Grizz was selling furs; by four, both sought and caught
Up in the actual building of this wonder of the age
And as director of a gold mine, move up to centre stage?
The pass must be explored at once, to decide if it might
Be what he was looking for and find if Grizz was right.

Growlerzoon Van Roarden needed to be certain beyond doubt,
And there was one way for sure for him to find that out.
He'd have to send a team in something like a dash,
Take a quick peep, and then out again. It was very rash.
For winter was a-coming, and he was desperate to know
Despite the risks they took of being caught up in the snow.
So first thing the next morning, with surveyors by his side,
Big Grizz was off to the mountain on his first railroad ride.
It was frightening and exciting to be travelling so fast;
It was all clink-clang and rocking as everything flashed past.
They rattled on for hours till at last they reached the gangs
Who were driving in the rail spikes with loud and rhythmic clangs.

Clambering from the train, they commandeered a cart
With equipment and provisions and straightway made a start,
And drove hard towards the clouds that both marked and hid from view
The mountain range until a break revealed a summit that he knew
Lay south, near the pass they looked for and needed to explore.
After three days of rough going, they entered the valley floor,
Hard work started, taking the cart as far as it would go,
Amid the rocks, boulders, and sprinklings of snow.
After that 'twas all on foot with packs upon their backs,
Climbing, crawling, clambering, and sorting out a track
That could be used to threadle through the tough terrain
If hacked and engineered, could be managed by a train.
Weather was getting nasty – made surveying impossible.
Snow and darkness made leaving quickly far more sensible.
Back to the cart and none too soon; the driver keen to leave
With them and baggage all aboard, he jostled up their steeds.
A blizzard chased them to the plains, where the snow turned into rain.
Searched for the smudge of smoke – pleased to see a train again!
A hot welcome, not just warm, a crowd of eager greetings,
All bursting to know the results around Van Roarden's meeting.

"Will it do? Can we get through?"
"If you're gunning for a fight?
"'Cos if you are the answers: YEP! Big Grizz sure got it right."
Caps flung high into the air with loud ecstatic yells,
A roar to make a lion proud, the engine's ringing bell.
Above it all, the whistle shrieked in triumphant blasts:
No long loops, no Indians – how it brightened up their tasks!
They carried the heroes from the cart, paraded shoulder high,
Swirling in a wild dance and laughed till fit to cry!

Steaming back to San Drego, in Van Roarden's den,
He studied the reports and assessing there and then.
The route required three tunnels, and what could cause some hassle
Was a major chasm that would need a massive trestle.
Surprising, the effect and speed of news a pass was found,
Stimulating shockwaves like an earthquake through the ground.
The heart of hard finance beat athletically and inspired
Plain Jane shares into things of ravishing desire.
Investors were pressed to invest and reinvest some more.
Company offices had besiegers squeezing through the doors.
The directors were delighted by the new state of affairs
And rightly presented Big Grizz with a handsome gift of shares.
The financial flow assured for materials they'd need,
Increase of the labour force moved the work at greater speed.
Track-laying veered toward the west, aiming for the pass.
A thorough survey could be done when spring would come at last.
From local gathered timber, the bridge builders made selections
That they prepared, cut, and fixed together into sections.
The rails raced across the wide expanse during wintertime,
By the spring thaw, Runny Nose was reached by the line.

It proved well-named, but never mind – they weren't doing bad.
They mustered their battalions and attacked with all they had.
Entering and pushing hard to carve out a slow incline,
In the easy lower levels, they were progressing fine.
The picks and shovels swung continually all day
Splitting rocks and boulders that stood in their way.
The pass echoed and re-echoed the explosions of gunpowder.
The tumbling of falling rocks rumbling even louder.
But the farther up the pass, the harder the endeavour,
Doing all they could to make the best use of the weather.
By the time its curtain fell closing down the show,
Work continued in the tunnels, regardless of the snow.

While the clamouring forced its way, and up to date with mapping,
Big Grizz was unneeded and ostensibly went trapping.
Only two knew his real motive was prospecting El Dorado.
As gentlemen, both kept that word incommunicado.
Neither being incontinent with a confidence,
A mutual trust developed that had its consequence.

In the plains, teams were engaged upon construction,
Preparing parts of trestle with which to span the chasm.
The tunnel's drilling and explosions were like cannon noise that rings.
Moles and beavers, placed as foremen, as they knew about such things.
At last they burrowed through and reached the chasm's side.
The sight was awesome, being very deep and wide.
Awful and impossible! Are trains to fly across the void?
The spring was late in coming, and Van Roarden was annoyed.

Standing at the tunnel's mouth, he sniffed a whiff of glory,
Swung back his head, and let rip a roar — defiant, loud, and gory.
His challenge proclaimed magnificence was destined to be here,
And all the labouring teams that heard responded with a cheer.
Snow was slow and was not to be rushed in melting clean away,
But at last turned into slush and brought that long-awaited day
That commenced with employment for the mountain goats,
With skills that they excelled in, poised on sheer-faced slopes:

Cutting ledges for the feet of the timber beams.
The pre-made parts were put in place by the bolting teams.
A hive of shinnying baboons amongst the swinging sections
Assembled all the many pieces that fitted to perfection.
It was broad-based on its footings, with towering, sloping sides
Till at the top, it narrowed to just one rail track wide.
Because the parts were standardized, work progressed apace,
So daring that the line seemed to leap out into space.
The conceived massive masterpiece, a most impressive sight,
Built with a descending slope and curving to the right
To take the tiny tread of rails to the far-off rocky ledge
From where the bed was clawed and cleaved into a mountain edge.
When completed, there came the time for trying out the trestles
By taking the first locomotive over the high metals.
Though the wildebeest selected had already made his will,
He chickened out last minute, and another filled the bill.
A shuff of steam, a careful start, gingerly at a crawl
For fear of derailment and that yawning, abysmal fall.
Creaks below the wheels caused stomach-churning throes,
But as the structure took the strain, 'twas, "Steady as she goes!"
Down the slope and to the bend, the part dreaded most,
Crawling slowly, safely on – how he now could boast!

The test deemed satisfactory, but there was trouble even worse:
He had to do it back again, this time in reverse!
After making it back safely and judging the cautious test,
The crew stepped down, hairs on end, and assessed it a success.
The feat had proved the structure sound. By way of gratitude,
Van Roarden gave his own gold watch, which he presented to
The engineer, who'd had the worst fright of his life.
The fireman was also given a nice something for his wife.
Now their way was opened, the route descending through
Runny Nose's other nostril, the pass's end in view.
Down to the welcomed flatlands of the western plains
Then straight for Wickyappelis, and their goal was gained,
Concluding that which some had said would never cross the summit.
They could scarce believe they'd been and gone and done it!
Apart from general tidying up and bits of titivations,
The next big job embarked upon was the list of invitations
To the official opening and the inaugural run.
'Twas four hard years since the great work had begun.

The San Drego and Wickyappelis line opened in grand style
That attracted large crowds drawn from many a mile.
Some came from as far away as the mailing stations
By the weekly stagecoach from Perlouk and Consternation
(Also known by their traducers as Puke and Constipation)
To find San Drego all decked out for the great occasion
With banners, flags, and bunting, igniting their imaginations.
Jostling excited folk in their best they kept for Sunday,
For glimpses of the chairdog and directors of the company.
Three bands playing different tunes, one with another vying,
Made it so hard to hear all the speechifying.
Amidst all this, Van Roarden received their congratulations.
Dainty parasols and flowery hats bobbed with expectations.
Standing tall: a gleaming locomotive, panting and alive.
Its front bore the chairdog's portrait with flags on either side
And garlanded about it like a sacrificial bull.
The engineer, when not tapping gauges, gave the bell a pull.
The great climbed graciously aboard, acknowledging the crowd.
The responsibility for this journey made its crew so proud.
Fascinated youngsters stood quizzing all the parts.
To be an engine driver the desire of their hearts.
Right on time, the whistle blew, telling crowds to stand aside.
Deafening, shrieking snorts of steam blew out gloriously wide.
As shiny rods started to move and slowly turn the wheels.
For those up close, the noise and smell were one of this life's thrills.
Thick smoke developed into a plume that lay above the train.
Spontaneous yells and cheers burst out as it took the strain.
Tough youngsters rode alongside, chasing it in hot pursuit,
Rooting and tooting with their guns with yells in wild salute.
Great sports of sheer high spirits. The train passengers delighted
Till, gaining speed, they pulled away, and waving hats departed.
Then back to town, to booze booths and to see the sights,
Getting tanked up for the hoedown to be held that night.

The important and the privileged socializing on the move,
Served with a convivial glass, and enjoyed the passing views.
Big Grizz, well-dressed and revered as expert on the pass,
Was more knowledgeable and loquacious with each successive glass.
Happily, the discussions of potentials of the line
Waxing very eloquent and rising to sublime.
Till time to halt and stretch their legs, now that they were able,
For a picnic champagne luncheon laid out on long tables.
Their comfiture completed, they were recalled to the train –
Refreshed, resumed their posturing, and on their way again.
Their expectancy was real enough of entering the pass
That had made this wonder possible, now to be seen at last.
The steady, rhythmic huff and chuffing as the loco' loped along,
Till entering the pass, it was compelled to change its song
To fierce staccato snorting as it began the climb
Through scenery declared by all as particularly fine.
All were enchanted by the pinewoods, riverbanks, and runnels.
Lamps were lit to reassure before they reached the tunnels.
The plunge into the first black hole, their vivacity was unsettled
With a loud increase of imprisoned noise and rumbling shrieks of metals.
Very brave in time of darkness – then emerging into light.
A quick view from higher up induced squeals of sheer delight.
A second tunnel swallowed them; noble was their indifference.
The conversations flowed conjointly with a marked persistence.
Another sudden flash of day and a most impressive view –
As the train made its upward way, the grandeur ever grew.
Now as seasoned travellers, a third tunnel of no note
Only caused a comment on the increasing reek of smoke.
Then without warning, from darkness into light
They were on the trestles, caught aghasted by the sigh
Of the spectacular vastness on unsupported space,
Crossing the void of the abyss at a fearful pace.
From the carriage windows, no trestle could be seen –
Instead, a sickening drop to chasm floor and nothing in-between.

'Twas fearfully disconcerting to look down on soaring eagles;
If only there were railings, it would help to stop the tingles.
Like hitting the underside of clouds, smoke went streaming by.
A frightened bison bellowed, "What're we doing in the sky?
"Is the damn fool of a driver aiming for the moon?"
Vertigo and affectation caused many then to swoon.
One fair gazelle suffered a fit of tizzwasic agitations
And fainted clean away; took tender ministrations of
Three handsome wolves to bring her round, where smelling salts had failed.
She was ever so indebted, while Aunty Lope just wailed.
Conductors rushed to close the curtains and pull down the blinds.
It became company policy to adjust them before times
The train reached a reassuring mountain, if only on one side.
The bison planned flasks in every pocket for the return ride.
"Get oblivious as a skunk, damn it! Cross it sober? Never!
"It might be Roarden's masterpiece, but its one unholy terror!"
With every mile down the pass, they confidence returned.
And amended their reactions, so raw truth was rather spurned.
Fainting became "breath-taking beyond all desiring";
Abject terror: "a quite wonderful experience, utterly inspiring."
Never again turned into "must not be missed at any price."
And so prepared themselves if asked, "Oh, it was really very nice!"
Feeling better about themselves, they could now enjoy the ride.
Racing across the open plains, and on time arrived,
Steaming into Wickyappelis to vast expectant crowds
Exuberantly welcoming these pioneers of the rails.
As the travellers alighted, a large band at the station
Played "See, the Conquering Hero Comes", favoured much on such occasions.
For the heady adulations, the tune "Doodle" caught the mood,
And why not? An untimely and a foul thing now to be a prude
On a day of great rejoicing; the great work had been done,
And anyone with any sense would want to join the fun.

After a decent milling, the local dignitaries withdrew.
The governor and senators lead their charming wives to
A banquet for the merchants and the bank's investors,
Provided without regard to cost by the company directors,
Assuaging appetites for addresses, toasts, and presentations.
Thereafter assessed the finest feast for a generation.
To conclude the bright festivities: a grand and glittering ball,
With swirling society flowers spoilt for choice of rich or tall!
Saluting of their partners, firm arms around the waists,
High prancing steps swept the floor at a lively pace.
Oh, what utter Joy!
A romantic end to a famous day; though exhausting, it was stunning,
Declaring the railroad now properly up and running.

Next morning, when Van Roarden met Big Grizz in the street,
He gently called him aside to somewhere more discreet.
Expressing earnest gratitude, there was no interruption
By registering his claim that would have halted the construction
Of the line. He requested a private word because
Was Grizz in favour of partnership? Which indeed he was.
He recommended he should register his claim, which indeed he did!
"Please, call me Growlerzoon."
"And you can call me Big."
Growlerzoon, meantime, at a bargain price acquired
The materials that the company no longer now required:
The invaluable and portable wooden tracker's sheds,
With useful shovels, picks, tents, bedding, and bunk beds.
Then he organized it's carting over mountains to the site,
And thus the core of Grizzville sprung up overnight!

As foreseen, news that a gold field had been struck
Brought prospectors in like flies to dig and try their luck.
When they arrived, they were all agreeably surprised
At the facilities available and so well organized.
Roarden's role was to ensure that all needs were supplied,
While Big Grizz was director overall and, as such, relied
Upon uniformed leopards to keep order and the law.
Many an old-timer had not seen the like before.
It was, of course, inevitable that news of such a strike
Attracted the attention of both good and bad alike.
In the latter category, there appeared two brothers,
Somewhat shady-looking characters, though perhaps no worse than others.

One was known as the Racoon Kid; the youngest, Black-Eyed Sid.
They had not come to do that which others did.
The Kid applied and got a job assisting in the store,
And Sid worked behind the bar and cleaning up the floor.
Both worked hard and nipped about, attentively snappy.
Doing their level best to keep their clients happy.
The two ears and just one mouth are a general facility;
But using them in that proportion is a rare ability.
Serving behind the counters, they heard all the news,
Were sympathetic to the problems, and agreed with all the views.
On the face of it, Kid and Sid passed as decent fellers
But deep down where it mattered they were crafty little beggars.
As the accrued deposits grew too large to hold,
Once a month, for safety's sake, guards transported gold
To the railroad halt in the pass before it was taken on by train
To the city's holding bank, where it would remain

Till season's end, thus lightening the prospectors job
Of protecting their hoard and risk of being robbed.

All the time, Grizzville grew, the store needed more room.
The simple bar was much enlarged, becoming the saloon.
A lot of work but worth it within a season's span:
A set-up that pretty well fulfilled the partners' plan.
Credit where all credit's due for making a success
And order out of the chaos that could have been a mess.
The two racoons bided their time to learn and note the reason
Why the last gold consignment was largest of the season.
The weather turned at last, bringing the first snow.
After closing down and boarding up, time to pack and go.
Whilst winter blew icy blasts blanketing the hills,
Further plans were being hatched for both good and ill.

The winter proved a long one, and thick snow hung about,
Till it shrunk into a gurgling thaw, and shoots of green burst out.
And like a shot, the lads were back, ready for the dig –
Boiling hot with eagerness, hoping to strike it big.
The saloon was ready for their pleasure and delight,
Hot basic meals all day and entertainments of a night.
Poker was played with imposed limits on the stakes,
Which saved furniture and fighting in the bar at any rate.
On Wednesday nights and Saturdays, they put on a show
That proved to be so popular that everyone would go

Just to see Lovely Luscious Lily, a cheetah who was able
To give them all a rousing turn as she mingled amidst the tables.
She would alight upon the bar with fancy, frilly kicks,
A sauntering sort of prowl with a waggle of the hips
And gave the lads the glad eye. There were some who thought
That in fact it was she who invented the catwalk.

She knew how to tease and sock it to 'em with a song.
They adored her: in their eyes, she could do no wrong.
Their opinion was well justified. As everybody's mate,
Despite her stagy ways, she always played it straight.
The only one that caused her instincts to have a qualms
Was Black-Eyed Sid, with feelings of repugnance and alarms.
Not that either showed their feelings; they were far too shrewd,
Both knowing there was nothing to be gained in being rude.
Luscious helped the lovelorn when they had to write
Letters that were dreamt on, under pillows, late at night,
Suggesting those turns of phrase to rouse a fainting heart
That kept the flame of love ablaze while sweethearts were apart.
And for this, oft times, she received a little gift of gold
That was prudently put aside for when a cat is old.
But that was by no means yet – Lil was in her prime
And therefore made the most of it while she still had time.
The chief cook was rather smitten and paid increased attention,
While others fancied themselves to vie for her affections.
Keeping up the balancing trick, she'd not commit to any.
'Twas best for trade and profits to keep everybody happy.

She ruled supreme as Grizzville's
queen: the cherry on their cake,
Glittering like the gold they sought
– the gem that helped to make
Grizzville prosperous and well run;
an undoubtable success,
While other gold fields rushes were a rapacious mess.

Big Grizz heard tell of a touring group
that had arrived by sea,
Who were performing in San Drego
as a theatric company.
When the loud acclaims abated, they
were due to storm the Grand.
And sure to knock Wickyappelis
flat with a three-week stand.
As Grizzville's door lay off their
route, a good remuneration
Promised on the nail secured
their theatrical sensation.
To bring the lads a bit of culture,
a taster of high art,
For most had never seen a play
or viewed a showman's cart!
It would be all so new to them;
they could do with being taught
Of life's finer things – or so
the thespians thought.
The company duly arrived and
laboured straight away,
Setting stage and scenery and sorting out the play.

Behind closed curtains for two days, rehearsals were directed.
Excitement mounted when news leaked out that it was suspected
Their own, their very own Luscious Lil was to play a part.
That fact alone would ensure a triumph from the start.
All seemed set for a success, the signs being auspicious.
The vehicle a melodrama; passions tender to malicious.
First night, the place was packed. The producer ask for shush!
That achieved, curtain up on a log cabin in the bush.
A widowed homestead mother with her good son, honest Jack.
Grinding poverty – times are hard, the outlook very black.
Enter Lil as daughter May, an outburst of yells and cheers!
Jack resolves to search for gold; he could be gone for years.
The curtain falls. Liquor all round to drink to the young man's health,
Admire his guts, and wish him well in searching for his wealth.
Act two: A storm is raging. Mother and daughter, all alone.
Loud knocking. They cry, "Who can that be, calling at our home?"
The door bursts open, and there stands the vile Gropey McApe.
He demands arrears of rent. They know there's no escape.
They cannot pay, they've nothing left – they plead. Has he no pity?
Instant eviction — Unless, of course . . . He moves towards poor Lily.
Uproar! The house went mad at her frightful situation.
One in front was so consumed by righteous indignation
To fix that low-down, two-timing, no-good son of a bitch,
Whipped out his gun and shot him – the final act was ditched.
General approval of the play, "'Cos he sure 'ad it comin'!"
Their Lil was safe, repute intact, saved from all his grubbing.
No one bothered that they saw if honest Jack's returned.
Lil and her mother's gratitude they had forever earned.
The company packed up overnight, fled to their next engagement,
Hoping to find some fool to be McApe's replacement.

Then of a sudden, that old nippy chill was in the air,
Announcing what was pending; it was time now to prepare
And make a start of closing down and packing up together
To get off Konnit Mountain before the heavy weather.
Most had at least found gold enough to justify the reason
For efforts considered, overall, a profitable season.
While this was going on, Big Grizz thought he ought
To take a last look at his traps to see what he had caught.
The furthest he had set them up was in the chasm's floor.
He already gathered five fine pelts and was checking now for more.
Flurries of snow had been swirling for at least two days;
The sky told of a blizzard that was on its way.
Then suddenly, clear clanking sounds echoed through the pass,
Clattering for some time and made him stop to ask,
"Whatever's that — tumbling rocks? No, it didn't sound like rumbling.
"It was definitely a ring of metal bouncing against something."
The more he thought about it, the less he understood.
It could not have been the trestle, as that was made of wood.
The only metal on the trestle was the rails —"The Rails!"
This compelled him to investigate. Had something up there failed?
He gathered up his catch of furs and made his way up to the trestle,
Knowing getting to the top was going to be a hassle.
The timber beams glistened, covered with snow and ice.
It being cold, he being old, the prospects where not nice.
His very recent prosperous-ness had added to his weight
And oft obliged him to stop in a gasping, breathless state.

The higher the more dangerous, the wind increasing to a gale,
Blowing hard with driving snow mixed with stinging hail.
It took a lot of hairy struggling, but at last he reached the top,
Where he still had to be careful, to avoid a dreadful drop.
The track it self was made of rails spiked to sleeper beams
That were laid across the bridge's width with large gaps in-between.
Perched on the top of slippery beams, the void on either side,
Big Grizz moved on all fours so that he would not slide
Off and in this manner, he edged his way to check the track.
Buffeted by the blizzard that tugged to blow him back,
He pressed on, finding nothing wrong till he reached the curve.
Creeping halfway round, he saw a sight to freeze his nerve.
He could scarcely believe his one eye: a rail had been replaced!
A few spikes were left to hold three lengths of soft wood in its place.
As it is the outer rail on curves that turns a train,
Consequently it's the one that takes the greatest strain.
"Of all the dirty, rotten, filthy, stinking things to do!
"I'd marmalize whoever's done this, if I but only knew."
The wickedness appalled him. "Who would derail a train
"And send all crashing down to death? They're hellishly insane!"
But what now? The next train out had the last consignment
Of prospectors and dear Lily for their wintertime retirement.
He could not get back to warn them of the trap that lay ahead,
So tried very hard to think straight for what to do instead.
If he stayed out where he was, he'd soon be covered white.
His only hope was the tunnel's mouth, and stand against the light.
He turned around most carefully and slowly started back
Like a crawling trapeze artist who had long since lost the knack.

Getting there was awful. The lofty views had disappeared;
Engulfed in driving whiteout, he had cause to be a feared.
He finally reached the tunnel mouth, relieved from wind and sleet
But racked with pain and glistening white, frozen nose and feet,
It was only than he realized he was stone cold to the core.
Beat his arms around his chest, jumped till his feet were sore.
The wind howled across the tunnel's mouth. What else could he hear?
It sounded like a train – It was! His stomach clenched with fear.
He took his stand to be best seen for saving life and limb,
Silhouetted at the entrance with the light behind him.
The faint chuffing sounded stronger, changing tone as it emerged
From the second tunnel with a rhythmic panting surge.
Chuffer-puffing, chuffer-puffing. "Yeah, it's definitely comin'!"
Chuffer-puffing catastrophically unto its doom, unknowing.
It entered into this tunnel and came clattering along.
Resolution turned to anguish as least all hope had gone.
In the far-off distance, he saw the head lamp's light,
Frantically jumped, and waved his arms as inspired by fright.
Would the crew see through the smoke and spot him up ahead?
If they did not, then it's for sure they would all be dead.
From the cab the view impaired by smoke and smarting smuts,
The engineer thought he saw a black blob going nuts.
Realizing it was someone trying hard to warn him,
He threw the valve gear in reverse, brakes upon wheel rims
Skidded protesting on the rails with ear-piercing shrieks.
The train juddering towards him like a Minotaur that freaked
Him out, pressing himself against the tunnel's side;
The deafening cacophony continued in its slide.

The cylinder caught his cuff and pulled him from the wall,
Dragged him from the tunnel and tossed him in lethal fall.
The train came to a stop, still not knowing what was wrong.
They rolled back into the tunnel, as the wind was very strong.
They waited till the blizzard passed and they could see ahead.
Whatever was the danger that caused him to be dead?
The trestle appeared well enough with its covering of snow,
So why delay? "Raise some steam, and let her gently go."

The only gold recovered was a nugget in his pocket.